Relatively Speaking

by
Mark Fletcher M.A.(Oxon)

Contents

Relatively Speaking

ISBN 1 898295 06 9

First published by English Experience   1991
Revised and reprinted   1994
© English Experience
Illustrations by Mark Fletcher
Printed in Great Britain by
Penton Printing, Canterbury, Kent CT1 3AP

Relatively Speaking
Acts 1 - 5
on Cassette
ISBN 1 898295 17 4

RELATIVELY SPEAKING - Your Course!

INTRODUCTION

Have you ever wanted to travel through time - and around the world- with complete freedom? **Relatively Speaking** is your passport to do that!

As you start this Course you become one of a team of people making a film about the key ideas and discoveries which have shaped our civilisation.

You will have the opportunity to contribute your own ideas and experiences, to work with others, and to do research on your own. It will be a stimulating and rewarding journey. Your first step is to choose a character from the page opposite. Your character (AA, EE, GG, MM, PP, TT) has a major role in the dramatised journey of **Relatively Speaking**.

Study Notes

* If you are using Relatively Speaking as a classbook you will probably be following the Teaching Notes on page 38.

* If you are working on your own

   1) Identify with one of the characters on page 3.

   2) Read through each unit and listen to the recorded version.
   (Cassette ISBN 898295 17 4).

   3) Spend some time on the language input. Use a dictionary; underline the "key phrases"; work through the "vocabulary hunt"; practice saying the "phonology specials".

   4) Let your imagination get to work in the "Using your senses" section. (Relax... make an "internal home movie" of each scene.)

   5) Collect/look at as much supplementary material as possible. The 'Ancilliary material' list on page 39 is a guide - and also check the context of events with the chart on page 40.

   6) Go back to the text to find answers to the "Can you explain..." section.

   7) Read/listen to the Act again and then use the picture 'memory map' as a basis for preparing a talk. Retell the information in the Act - and use phrases from the text in your talk.

Dr Jacob Bronowski's book 'The Ascent of Man' (ISBN 0 563170 64 6) and also the BBC TV series of that name make excellent support material.

An important Study Point.

The more you contribute to the story through using your imagination, experience and knowledge, and bringing in appropriate pictures and objects, the more you will enjoy and benefit from the rich treasury of language and information the Course offers.

The title of the Course is a play on words. There is a sense in which we are all *relatives* of one another. Ideas all have a *relative* value. We pay tribute to Einstein's great theory of *relativity*. And, of course, we'll do a lot of *speaking*.

And now you're ready to set off for the plains of East Africa! Don't forget a sun hat. Have a good trip!

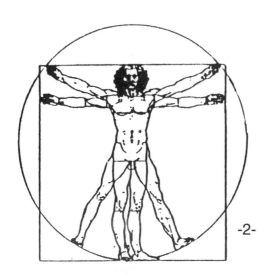

RELATIVELY SPEAKING

These are the members of a team producing a film on key stages in the development of civilisation .

First name	Family name	Profession	Description	Personal Information
	Archway	*Architect, Builder.*		
	Engineoil	*Engineer Mathematician, Physicist.*		
	Greenfingers	*Gardener, Botanist.*		
	Marketplace	*Merchant,*		
	Penandink	*Painter, Writer.*		
	Timpani	*Theatre Director Musician.*		

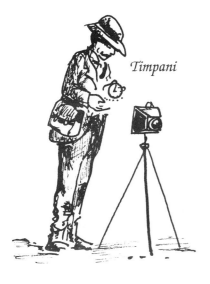

RELATIVELY SPEAKING

Act 1

Scene 1   East Africa

EE   You've chosen to start us off here, Greenfingers.
Can you explain why?

GG   Certainly. The sun is beating down,
and the heat makes the horizon shimmer.
There's not a great deal to see now, is there?
But this savannah country,
stretching out along Lake Rudolph like a ribbon,
is the navel of the world!

TT   I take it you mean this is where the story of man begins?

GG   Well, here in the layers of volcanic ash of two million year ago,
we find the fossils of the creature who was to become man.
Human evolution began in the great rift valley of Northern Kenya
when the African climate changed to drought,
and man first put his foot on the ground and walked upright.

AA   Isn't it fascinating that fossils show so little change in animals,
but so much change in man.

GG   Perhaps we can account for that by looking at
what physical gifts man shares with the animals,
and what makes him different.

PP   Phew! It's like an oven!
How about walking over to the shade? . ... That's better.

GG   Take an athlete, a pole vaulter, for example.
As he prepares to jump the heart beat goes up
and chemicals get energy for the blood by burning sugar
- just like an animal.
The difference lies in the way the athlete plans actions in advance,
deliberately preparing, and seeing the jump in his imagination.
It's this foresight that releases the brake on evolution!
Let me give you some evidence of that ....

MM   Hold on. All this highbrow stuff is making me hungry.
Any chance of a snack?
A coffee and hamburger would suit me.

TT   That's a good example of man having the same basic needs as the animals!

GG   But it also ties in nicely with what I was going to say.
Stone tools for striking and cutting
demonstrate a huge leap of skill and foresight.

EE   More than a million years ago one of my relatives
must have been the first technologist!

T T   Every animal leaves traces of what it was.
Only man leaves traces of what he has created.

AA   Talking of animal traces, - look at these paw prints.
I'm pretty sure a pride of lions has used this spot for a siesta!

EE   Imagine my early ancestor sitting just here in the dust
and realising his hands had new power because of a tool!

GG   Somewhere in the last million years or so,
biological refinements in the brain-centres that control the hands,
led to a refinement in toolmaking.
Look at your own hands and see what I mean.
Touch the tip of your thumb with the tip of your index finger.
There - no ape can do that!

EE   Do you see how Penandink is holding that pencil to sketch?
That ability to manipulate objects with such precision
is a clue to the speed of evolution of man.

PP   Look at the play of light and shade on the valley side .....

MM   What were you saying about hamburgers and evolution just now?

GG   I can give you that bit of the jigsaw.
The early apes and humanoids spent their time
rummaging for vegetarian food.
From about two million years ago the family of man began to eat meat.

TT   What difference did that make?

GG   It gave a much higher protein intake,
so it cut down the time spent eating by two thirds!
The far reaching effects of this were to give time for planning.

MM   'Planning' initially meant 'hunting strategies.'
The spin off from this is that people learned to work together,
and this provided a huge impetus for that vital human attribute,
the development of language.

AA   Timpani. Do you want to say anything about music at this stage?

TT   We can only speculate on how animal grunts become language,
but I'd like to think that my ancient relatives took pleasure
- or at least a feeling of fellowship,
from that first, ritual, rudimentary dancing, and chanting.

AA   Let's have a look at this map.
These early humans moved prodigious distances in search of food.
I'll show you. A million years ago, North Africa.
Seven hundred thousand years ago, Java.
Four hundred thousand years ago they fanned out
to reach China in the East and Europe in the West.

MM   Hunters adopted new strategies following the herds of reindeer,
- as the Lapps still do today, -
using wild animals as a kind of walking larder.

EE   It's so hot and dry here it's hard to imagine snow,
let alone the impact of the three great Ice Ages.

PP   You're right. I suggest we make a move which will help us . . .

Scene 2 The Mountains of Spain

TT   This is very different! The edge of the ice sheet.

EE   Thank goodness it's the end of the ice age not the beginning!
Human beings survived the Ice Ages
partly because of another master discovery, the use of fire.

PP   Let's take a look inside one of these caves.
Follow me ... I don't think the owners are at home!
Here at Altamira, and in the caves of the Dordogne in France,
we have a wonderful insight into the minds of our early relatives.

GG   Careful ..... mind your head..... shine the torch over here...

PP   There! Think about this for a moment.
Man had to invent flint tools, and weapons.
Those are scientific developments essential to survival.

AA   But why add to these, the arts that now astonish us?

PP   Look at the animation, the power of line,
those bison flanks quivering with life.

MM   And why, above all, are these wonderful paintings
not in the places where he lived
but in the dark, secret, hidden, inaccessible recesses of the caves?

EE   Magic?

AA   Probably, yes - but what magic did the hunters
believe they got from the paintings?

PP   Possibly these pictures express that same power of anticipation
we talked about with our athlete earlier.

GG   Here, in the sudden glare of the torch flame
the hunter would see the wild animals as he would see them in the hunt.

PP   The painter has caught a moment of fear and exhilaration
to test and prepare the nerve.
We look at these pictures as if they were a glimpse of the past.
For our ancestors, I suggest, they were a peephole to the future!

MM   What we're saying is that science and art are both uniquely human,
and derive from the same ability to visualise the future
and anticipate it.

TT   And look at the wall over there - those hand prints
of twenty thousand years ago.

PP   They are a statement of identity.
They speak to us over the millennia and say,
"This is my mark. This is Man!"

AA   Time for our third change of scene.
Careful as you back out of the cave . . .
we're off to the Garden of Eden - still, I'm afraid,
a symbol of the Fall of Man.

Scene 3 The Middle East

MM   It's not the paradise I imagine as Eden!

GG   No, but here about ten thousand years ago,
at the end of the Ice Ages, Spring replayed itself.
There was a quiet explosion
which marks the point at which civilisation takes off.

TT   That's an exciting claim. How are you going to justify it?

GG   Here in the fertile crescent of the Middle East
the nomadic way of life, where nothing is permanent,
gave way to settling in villages,
and that was made possible by a strange and secret act of Nature.

EE   Take a look at this ancient flint sickle.
It was found at Jericho - the oldest city in the world.

AA   And what does it mean? - I can see you're bursting to tell us.

GG   Pick an ear of wheat everyone ...
rub it through your fingers ... smell it.
In that burst of new life following the Ice Ages
a kind of wild wheat crossed with natural goat grass
and formed a fertile hybrid with twenty eight chromosomes-
much plumper than either of its antecedents with fourteen.
Then in a second 'genetic accident', Emmer as it is known,
crossed with another wild grass
to produce a still larger hybrid with forty two chromosomes
- and that's bread wheat - with a full ear of grain.

EE   Now, this is the extraordinary thing.....
an ear of wheat is so tight that it can't break up
in the wind to scatter and re-sow itself.

GG   So just as man rejoices that wheat was made to supply him
with sufficient food,
the wheat thinks <u>man</u> was made to help <u>it</u>,
because only with man's help can it propagate itself!

PP   A true fairy tale of genetics.

MM   Wheat and water make civilisation.
Jericho was old when Joshua brought its walls tumbling down.

GG   The Old Testament from Abraham onwards illustrates clearly
the change from a nomadic to a settled way of life.
Settled agriculture creates the conditions for technical progress
from which science accelerates.

EE   The needle, the pot, the spade, the loom, the harness, the plough....
I could name a hundred such inventions of the time and not
stop for breath.

MM   While we're here, look out at the green lands between the Tigris
and Euphrates.
Let's spare a thought for the toiling generations of our relatives
who gave so much to us from this, the cradle of our civilisation.

EE   I agree, and I don't want to break in on your meditations too rudely,
but time is moving on and there are other things
we really should take a look at while we're in this part of the world.
The step beyond simple agriculture was the domestication of animals.

PP   Look around - a flock of goats over there ..... sheep following
a shepherd .....
and see there, the draught animals, a heavily laden donkey
plodding down the dusty track,
and, like a snapshot from six thousand years ago,
two oxen pulling a plough in the field by the river's edge.

GG   Our relatives harnessed the power of these animals
to provide a surplus of production over consumption.

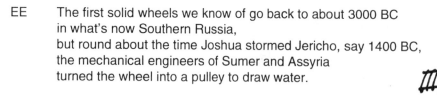

PP   Talking about food, is anyone else feeling peckish?

GG   Just a moment, hold your horses!
Then there's still the wheel to mention.

EE   The first solid wheels we know of go back to about 3000 BC
in what's now Southern Russia,
but round about the time Joshua stormed Jericho, say 1400 BC,
the mechanical engineers of Sumer and Assyria
turned the wheel into a pulley to draw water.

TT   Would anyone like to join me for a drink?
Lend a hand to turn the handle at this well.
The bucket goes down, down, down - splash!

AA   Some ancient wells are as deep as a hundred metres!

TT   Turn the handle again - up comes the bucket.
Clear, cool water splashing over us. Wonderful!
Water to drink, to wash and refresh ourselves,
to irrigate the parched fields and grow crops.

EE   The wheel and axle become the double root from which
invention grows, transmitting energy for carrying, pulling, grinding.

MM   The struggle continued between the settlers who produce
and the raiders who steal,
and agricultural societies reeled from time to time
from attack by the nomadic tribes of Asia.
The highly organised mobile hordes of Ghengis Kahn
pillaged their way from China to Central Europe in relatively recent times.
But wells, and access to water supplies,
irrigation, planting and harvesting,
these imply a regulated community life,
and these mark the emergence of civilisation as we know it.

PP   Do you see how the sky is turning violet and the first stars are coming out?

AA   I think we've made an excellent start, don't you?
We've covered a lot of ground in our first visits.

TT   Let's digest all that information
and decide how to use it in our film!

A photographic tricycle for tourists[1885]

Act 1
Key phrases   Find and underline :-

I take it you mean...
Isn't it fascinating...
The difference lies in the way...
Let me give you some evidence of this...
It also ties in nicely with what I was going to say...
Talking of...
What were you saying about...?
The far reaching effects...
The spin-off from this...
I suggest we make a move...
What we're saying is...
How are you going to justify it ?
Let's spare a thought for...
We've covered a lot of ground...

Phonology specials

The sun is beating down, and the heat makes the horizon shimmer.
Thank goodness it's the end of the ice age , not the beginning!
Careful...mind your head...shine the torch over here.
A heavily laden donkey plodding down the dusty track.
Would anyone like to join me for a drink?

Vocabulary hunt Find phrases in the text for ...

He uses a long stick to jump high -
Very intellectual (and a little snobbish) -
A game where you fit pieces together -
The opposite of a 'settled way of life' -
It happened around 1400 BC? -

Using your senses

Experience the heat and glare of the African plain at midday - and the welcome relief of shade. Feel the weight of a stone cutting tool in your hand. Visualise the wide plain and the herds of animals.

Feel the bitter cold. Bend low to enter the cave. Touch the rough walls. Imagine being the first person to shine a torch into the dark and discover these amazing pictures.
Look at the green of the irrigated land contrasting with the dry dusty desert. Listen to the flocks of sheep and goats going to be watered. Use your strength to draw water from the well and feel refreshed as it splashes on your skin.

"Hands on" experiences..

Have a good look at your "Materials collection" (see the list page 39)
How about making a stone cutting tool?
Make your own cave painting.
Take a close look at an ear of wheat.

Excuse me.
Can you explain.

i) the significance of GG's point about the thumb and index finger?

ii) how the change from a hunter gathering society to a farming society came about?

Mini role plays

i) AA and PP - you are stone age estate agents. Conduct some potential buyers around one of your properties explaining all its advantages.

ii) You are early advertising/marketing people. In pairs, choose one of the inventions mentioned in Scene 3. Present it to potential customers who, of course, have never seen such a wonderful thing before. Make sure they appreciate how it will revolutionize their life-style, and see if you can get some orders!

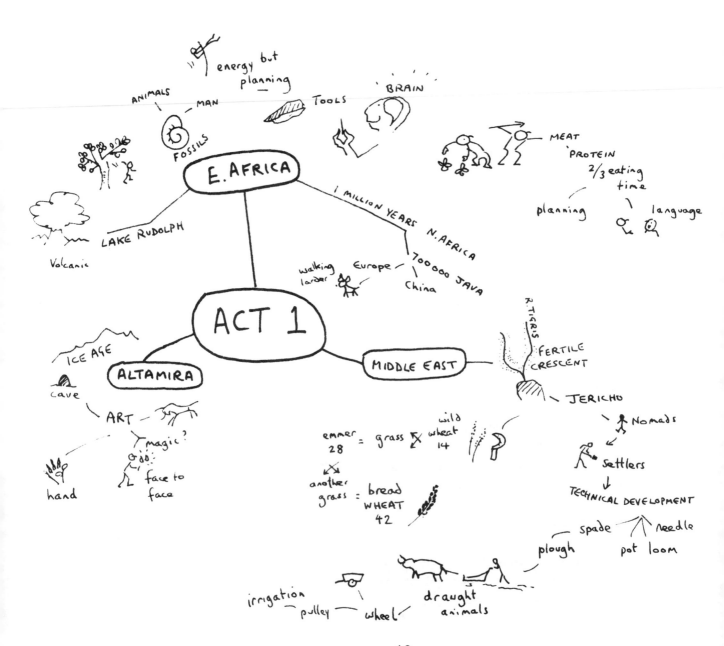

Act 2

Scene 1 The Island of Samos

AA   Can you pass me the grapes? Thanks.

TT   Any more retsina anyone?

EE   Not for me thanks. I'm beginning to feel pleasantly drowsy.

PP   Don't nod off just yet.
There's a lot to experience around here.
The gentle murmur of bees amongst the wild flowers,
and what a beautiful variety of flowers there are, pink, white, blue.

EE   I must say it's something of a relief to have reached this point.
What we saw of Egypt was fascinating and impressive, wasn't it?
Four thousand years of sculpture, solid, enduring,
expressing the traditions of a community.

GG   But essentially static!

AA   Do you remember what we saw at Karnak?
The great temples, the monuments, the carving
were an expression of the desire to overcome death,
pretending that in some way we just carry on as before.

GG   You're the expert Penandink. What did you think?

PP   What I enjoyed most were the minor arts.
The things made for daily use, and the wall paintings
that showed scenes from daily life.
  They had charm, elegance, even tenderness.

MM   It makes you realise what an era of restless change **we** live in.
The Egyptians handed on their symbols from generation to generation.
What did you feel about the monuments of Sumer and Babylon?

PP   First of all, amazement
that such massive figures and such a virile civilisation
should have been completely lost until the 1840's.
Then perhaps a little fear.
This is royal art to demonstrate power.

TT   Did you notice the way that, unlike Egyptian art,
there are no women shown in the Assyrian reliefs?

MM   What both of those civilisations did do though
was to develop the city as the central focus of community.
and develop means of communications to govern vast empires.

AA   I was given this clay tablet by the museum curator.
Careful ! Don't drop it. It's been around a long time!

MM   Sumerian cuneiform tablets and Egyptian hieroglyphics
provide a remarkable history of political events,
the daily records of administration, and personal communication.

PP   None the less, for me, it's like a breath of fresh air
to be on a Greek hillside .....
lizards scampering across the fluted marble of fallen columns
and Homer's wine dark sea beyond.
You might almost expect to hear Orpheus and his lyre
or see Icarus and Daedalus winging too near the sun.

MM   So much of what we take for granted first blossomed here.
Democracy of course, what a remarkable step forward that is!

PP   Samos is a magical island.
The air is full of sea and trees and music.

TT   I'd like to take a relative of mine, Pythagoras
as an example of what Greece has given us.
Pythagoras was a kind of magician to his followers
because he taught them that Nature is commanded by numbers.
There's a harmony in nature, he said, a unity in her variety,
and it has a language; numbers are the language of Nature.

GG   Sitting here in the sunshine, Nature seems very sensuous
and not at all numerical.

TT   Well, let me explain. Born about 580 BC,
Pythagoras found the basic relation between musical harmony
and mathematics. A single string vibrating produces a ground note.
The notes that sound harmonious with it
are produced by dividing the string into an exact number of parts.
Into exactly two, into three, into four.

EE   Pythagoras proved the world of sound is governed by exact numbers.
He went on to prove the same thing is true of the world of vision.

MM   Are you talking about his famous theory of the square on the hypotenuse?
I remember struggling with that at school, don't you?

AA   Don't let anyone tell you geometry is dull or irrelevant.
The Egyptians and Babylonians knew about right angles
in a practical, building, sense .

EE   Pythagoras had the genius to ask 'Why?'
Why is it that if we turn a triangle four times at right angles
it finishes in the same position?
Pythagoras raised knowledge from empirical fact to proof.
In my opinion, his theorum is the most important in all mathematics
because it penetrates the harmony of Nature.
It establishes in numbers the laws that bind the universe.

GG   You've certainly lifted a page from the maths book
and given it the glamour of a step in the ascent of man!

EE   Thanks, and here's a very human touch.
Did you know that when Pythagoras proved his great theorum
he offered a hundred oxen to the Muses as thanks for the inspiration?
A classic gesture of pride and humility that every research scientist feels
when the numbers dovetail and he can say
'This is a part of, a key to, the structure of Nature herself.'

AA   After that lecture you deserve a rest - and another drink.

PP   It's interesting that we have a tendency to think of Greece as
looking West.

AA   That's natural. As we've said before,
so much of Western civilisation comes from Greece.

MM   And Greece is very much a member of the European Economic Community.

PP   Even so, we shouldn't forget that in classical times
Greece looked Eastwards.

TT   The thought that inspired Greece flowed from Asia Minor,-
and it flowed back in that direction again
before it ever reached Western Europe.

EE   Euclid's 'Geometry' - until modern times the world's second best seller,
and Ptolemy's scheme of the universe went from Alexandria into Asia.

GG   Is everyone feeling rested and refreshed?
I'm sure we'll be back in these parts again
but now it's time for a change of continent,

and attitude - and altitude!

Scene 2 Peru   Macchu Picchu

TT   From the high snow-clad ranges of the Andes,
we can gaze down on the lost city of the Incas.

PP   It seems the most natural thing to take some clay, like this,
and mould it into a ball, a little clay figure, a cup, a hut.
We feel that the shape has been given to us by nature.

EE   Actually, nothing new is discovered about Nature
in the moulding of these warm, rounded shapes.
But there is another action of the human hand that is different and opposite.
That is the splitting of wood or stone
where a tool explores beneath the surface
and becomes an instrument of discovery,
the beginning of theoretical science.
From early times man made tools by splitting stone,
cleaving along the grain, revealing inner structure.
This discovery of underlying order makes it possible to take apart,
and put together in new arrangements.

GG   That's an interesting point.
The fundamental particles make nuclei, the nuclei join in atoms,
the atoms join in molecules, the molecules join in bases,
the bases direct the assembly of amino acids,
the amino acids join in proteins.

MM   Somehow we recognise a natural sense of hierarchy, layer on layer.
Human beings join in families, families join in kinship groups,
kinship groups in clans, clans in tribes, tribes in nations.

AA   Or, look at what's in front of us for example.
Stones make a wall, walls make houses, houses make streets,
and streets make a city.

MM   A city is stones, and a city is people.
But it's not just a heap of stones and not just a jostle of people.
It's a community organisation based on division of labour
and chains of command.

EE   There's a chilly wind at eight thousand feet. Wrap up well
and look at the way these stones have been cut.
Granite blocks cut to such accuracy that no mortar is needed.

MM   And this deserted, silent, city of 1500 speaks to us of every city.
First, supplies. On the steep, green, terraces
they grew the maize and potatoes to support the population.
Exactly as in the Fertile Crescent, it's the control of water that matters.

AA   The Inca irrigation system runs through the canals and aquaducts,
down into the desert and makes it flower.

MM   To sustain an empire, Egypt, Mesopotamia, Inca, or any other,
      takes a strong central authority.
      Three inventions support the network of authority.
      Roads, bridges, messages.

GG   These three are vital - they are always the first target of revolution.

MM   We know the Inca gave them much care, yet
      on the roads there were no wheels,
      under the bridges were no arches,
      and the messages were not in writing.
      The society was a pyramid. Everyone worked for one man, the Inca.

TT   It was an extraordinarily brittle empire, destroyed overnight
      by a hundred and six foot soldiers, and sixty two terrible horses.
      The work of the goldsmiths, the potters, the coppersmiths, the weavers,
      everything has gone. Only the work of the masons remains.

AA   And here is a measure of the time lag between the New World
      and the Old...
      The sixteenth Century Inca builders worked to the end of the empire
      using beams.
      They never invented the arch.

PP   And that's exactly the point the Greeks reached two thousand years earlier,
      and at which they also stopped.

EE   Can you picture a beam lying across two columns?
      A computer analysis shows the stresses on the beam increase
      as we move the columns apart.
      The longer the beam, the greater the compression, the greater the tension.
      As you know, stone is weak in tension and will fail at the bottom
      unless the columns are close together.

PP   Greek temples may look light and airy as the ruins lie open to the sky.
      Actually they are crowded avenues of pillars.

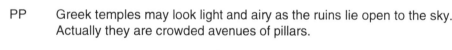

GG   The Greeks were fascinated by geometry, so it's strange they never
      invented the arch, isn't it?

AA   Perhaps it's not so strange. That invention
      was left to a much more practical, down to earth, culture.

Scene 3   Southern Spain - Segovia

TT   All this globe trotting's making me quite dizzy.
      Where are we now?

AA   I'm sure you'll recognise that familiar landmark.

TT   It's splendid ! Out all of proportion to its function of carrying water....

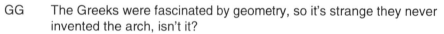

MM   But that's because we get water by turning a tap!
      It's easy for us to forget
      the universal problems of city civilisations.
      Every advanced culture depends on the kind of invention and organisation
      this Roman aquaduct expresses.

PP   I'm hazy about dates and dimensions.
      Can you put us in the picture a bit more?

AA   It was built about AD 100 in the reign of the Emperor Trajan
      and brings water from about ten miles away.
      The aquaduct spans the valley for almost half a mile
      in more than a hundred double-tiered round arches
      made of rough hewn granite blocks,
      laid without lime or cement.

TT   So, in engineering terms,
      what's the big advantage of the arch over the beam?

AA   The arch is a method of spanning space
      which doesn't load the centre more than the rest.
      The stress flows outward fairly equally throughout.
      So an arch can be made of separate parts, or blocks,
      which the load compresses.

EE   In this sense, the arch is a triumph of the intellectual method
      we talked about earlier at Macchu Picchu.
      The human ability to take nature apart
      and put the pieces together again in new and powerful combinations.

PP   Well, we've certainly got plenty to take apart and rearrange
      as a result of our travels so far.

GG   We've moved rapidly from ape-like relatives with flints
      to city states and Roman arches.
      I wonder what's in store for us next .....

Act 2   Key phrases Find and underline :-

Do you remember what...?
It makes you realise what...
Did you notice the way that...?
So much of what we take for granted...
A remarkable step forward...
We have a tendency to think...
We shouldn't forget...
The most natural thing in the world...
Can you picture...?
A much more practical, down to earth, culture...
I'm hazy about...
In engineering terms...
I wonder what's in store...

Phonology specials

The gentle murmur of bees amongst the wild flowers.
Careful! Don't drop it. It's been around a long time.
There's a chilly wind at eight thousand feet.
Wrap up well and look at the way these stones have been cut.
Roads, bridges, messages. These three are vital.

Vocabulary hunt

Complete the following:-

Don't...just yet.

It's like...air.

Don't let anyone tell you.....................................

We have.....................................as looking West.

The high.....................................of the Andes.

All this..........................is making me...................

Using your senses

Listen to the drowsy hum of the bees in the Spring warmth. Enjoy the rich, sweet, taste of grapes. Notice the quick, darting, movement of the lizards on the fallen marble columns and the variety of delicate flowers. Handle the clay tablet carefully. Let your thumb run over its surface.

You are high in the Andes. There's a chilly wind. Look down on the huge blocks of stone. Run your finger along the joins and admire the workmanship. Do you feel melancholy that so little remains of this civilisation?

"Hands on" experiences...

Have a good look at your "Materials collection".
Draw some triangles. Can you demonstrate Pythagoras' theorem?
Make some plasticine / clay figures, and experience this 'moulding' action.
Can you construct an arch out of everyday materials to see how much
weight it can carry?

To discuss.   Should subjects like mathematics, chemistry, art, religion, geography be taught completely separately at school or can they be connected?

Excuse me. Can you explain...   why EE put such emphasis on the 'splitting of wood or stone' and on 'the arch'?

Mini role plays

i) MM and GG. You are a Public Relations team representing the Inca Empire. Explain the great developments you have instigated and appeal to the United Nations for help against a rumoured invasion by Europeans.

ii) The year is AD99. TT - You are the Emperor Trajan. Get your architect and engineer to explain what they're going to do about the fact that it's midsummer and you can't have a bath because there isn't any water!

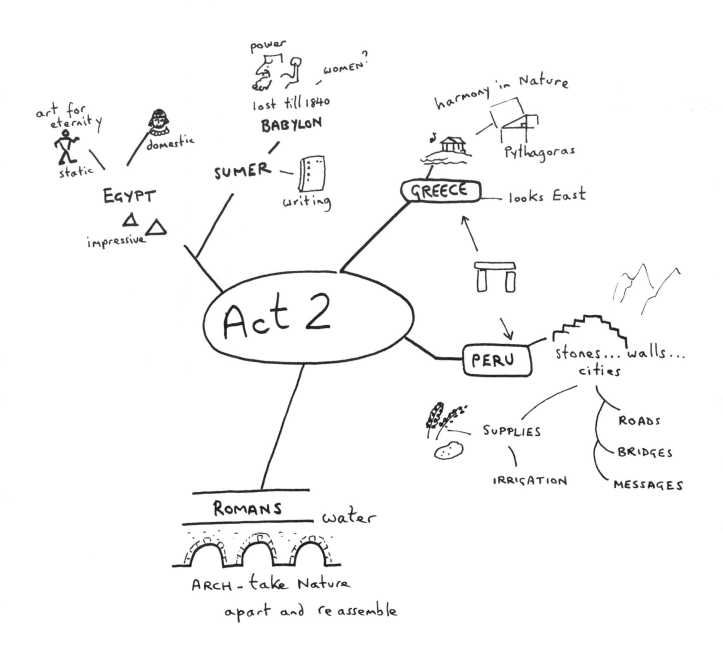

Act 3

Scene 1   China - The Great Wall

GG   The only man-made object visible from the moon!

MM   As you stand here a chill wind from the Steppes
pushes and pulls you every way.
The hot line of defence against the Tartar hordes!

TT   "A Tartar horn tugs at the north wind.
Thistle Gate shines whiter than the stream.
The sky swallows the road to Kokonor.
On the Great Wall, a thousand miles of moonlight".

AA   Let your eye follow the long winding line
till it disappears in the distance.
Here, hundreds of years before even the Great Wall,
was the high period of Bronze, the Shang dynasty before 1500 BC.

PP   Can you pass me that bronze vessel, please?
Have you ever handled anything like this before?
Run your finger over that fascinating detail - the interlocking patterns.

GG   It's certainly heavy. What was it used for?

PP   This is a ceremonial object - half playful, half divine.
The Shang for the first time created some sort of
unitary state and culture in China.
Bronzes like this are an expression of beauty, utility,
mastery and devotion to the craft.

EE   You'd agree that all cultures use fire for warmth, protection,
clearing woodland and so on?
Even more importantly for us, the use of fire reveals
a whole new class of materials, the metals.

MM   Certainly by 5000 BC copper was being smelted in Persia and Afghanistan.
From that point, our relatives went on to make metal
the backbone of civilised life.

EE   Copper can be moulded, hammered, cast, drawn,
and used for tools, ornaments and vessels.

TT   But, it's too soft to take an edge, isn't it?
As soon as it's put under strain
it visibly begins to yield.

AA   That's right. The ascent of man stood poised at the next step!
In the last fifty years or so we've come to understand about atoms and crystals.
We know that if we can introduce some gritty crystals
into copper's smooth parallel planes
this will stop the planes sliding under pressure,
and make the metal hard.

EE   By luck - or experiment - our ancient relatives - the coppersmiths
found just this solution too.
Amazingly, when you add an even softer metal, tin, to copper,
you form an alloy which is harder than either, bronze.

TT   Copper, bronze, ... and did the use of iron come next?

EE	Yes. Iron was first worked in its natural form, it arrives on the surface of the earth in meteorites. and the Sumerian name means 'metal from heaven'. As copper comes of age in its alloy, bronze, so iron comes of age in its alloy, steel.
MM	Steel was being made in India by about 1000 BC, but it remained a rare and limited material till recently.
EE	Very briefly, that's the story of alloying useful metals, which gave our relatives ever more efficient tools.
GG	Again, you see, the developments come from the leap of imagination that takes nature apart, then rearranges the parts to make new properties.
MM	While we're on the subject of metals we should mention the one that's exercised the strongest grip on human imagination. Gold for greed, for splendour, for adornment, for eternity. How many of us are wearing gold? The Spaniards plundered the New World in their eager search for it.
PP	Gold is the universal prize in all countries, cultures and ages.
T T	The Chinese put their finger on what makes it irresistible. Ko-kung said 'yellow gold, if melted a hundred times, will not be spoiled.'
AA	I don't know about you, but this wind is cutting through me like a knife. Let's head back to Europe, for another symbol of eternity.

Scene 2   France - the Cathedral of Rheims

AA	This way, just down this cobbled street.
GG	Mmm. Smell that!
AA	Come on, no stopping yet for croissants! There, look at that for an expression of the human spirit. The human spirit in search for harmony with the immortal. Of all the monuments to human effrontery there's nothing to match these towers of tracery and glass that burst into the light of Northern Europe before the year 1200.

GG	The vision and courage of our builder relatives is amazing.
TT	Lift the latch, push open the heavy door. The hinges creak. Our footsteps echo in the nave. Specks of dust hang dancing in the shafts of light.
PP	Gaze upwards. It's breathtaking, isn't it?
AA	The key invention is a new form of arch, not based on the circle, but on the oval. Dramatically, this takes the load off the walls . The stress flows through the arch to the pillars, and into the external supporting half arch.
GG	That's called a flying buttress, isn't it? And it means that the walls no longer support the weight of the building?

flying buttress

AA   That's right. You've been doing your architecture homework!
      As a result, the walls can be pierced to let in light.

EE   How high would you say this vault is?

AA   I'm not exactly sure. I'd guess a hundred and twenty or so feet.

PP   Spot on. I've got the guide book here. It says a hundred and twenty five.

GG   What's that in metres - about forty two, isn't it?

AA   Looking at this vast building you can feel that unique human delight.
      The pushing forward of skill beyond known limits.

PP   I'm sure the wandering builders,
      those intellectual aristocrats of the Middle Ages,
      must have felt that excitement when they knew their calculations were right
      and that the towering arches would stand.

TT   Listen. Around us are the echoes of Gregorian chant -
      the brothers at prayer.
      Plain song - beautiful, impressive, some say monotonous.
      Written down in individual musical short hand by choir masters.

PP   Look at the colours of that window - especially the deep blues!
      Can you imagine the impact of this story-telling in glass?

MM   And the impetus to a new industry!
      The glass burners worked day and night to supply the demand
      and these treasures were transported all over Europe.

TT   Europe was probably more internationally minded at that time, I suppose,
      than it has been before or since.
      Nations, in our sense, didn't really exist.

EE   Craftsmen travelled from region to region learning and practising their trade.

GG   Then something horrible and totally unforeseen happened.
      The Black Death swept over Europe killing one in four.
      Fear affected people's minds.
      No one travelled. Nationalism grew.

PP   The lovely flowering of early Gothic lost its way ...
      - but something very beautiful is waiting for us.
      We're off to Italy.

Scene 3   Florence

TT   I must say, this is one of my favourite cities.

GG   Let's stroll back over the Ponte Vecchio
      and drink in the atmosphere.

MM   One fascinating aspect of civilisation
      is the way the achievements of science and art
      relate to the political and economic realities of life.

EE   Why did things take off with Gothic in the twelfth century?

MM   Because the great restlessness of the Crusades was at an end.
      There was political stalemate between Moslem and Christian.
      International trade was being re-established,
      and there was more money around!

AA   Building land in Mediaeval walled cities was at a premium.
      So how did they build? - Upwards, of course.

      -20-

MM   Look at the position of Florence a couple of hundred years later.
The town had benefitted by being a junction on the way to Rome.
It was doing very well from the wool trade.
With a great deal of enterprise,
it had used the Northern plains of Italy as a manufacturing base
for the very profitable silk business,
and so became one of the richest towns of Mediaeval Europe.
A few quick witted citizens made fortunes from currency deals and banking.

silk

GG   Luckily for all of us these great merchant princes
turned out to be remarkable patrons of the arts!

PP   I suggest we settle down at that cafe under the colonnade
and get some coffees or ices
and talk about two people
whose spirits contribute so much to the Renaissance.

TT   Ah, that's better. There's room at these tables.
Move round a bit so we can all fit in.

GG   I've bought some lovely postcards from the stand over there.
It's about time I got in touch with some present day relatives!

AA   Can I see? Ah - the Baptistry, with its glorious mosaics.

EE   Glorious, yes. But severe.

PP   Representatives of a religion governed by remote authority,
the fixed images of the Byzantine world.

TT   While we're waiting for a waiter
it's worth reminding ourselves that, for the most part,
the knowledge of the Greeks and Romans passed Eastwards to Alexandria
and later to the great Islamic Empire of Baghdad
which stretched from Spain to China.

MM   While Europe hacked itself to pieces during the Dark ages,
Arab mathematicians, poets, artists, astronomers
created a world of autocratic elegance and delight.

GG   Some knowledge of this filtered back through the crusades.
One of my early relatives returned from campaigning
with the totally new concept of making a garden!

MM   We think of Italy, here, as the birth place of the Renaissance
but the conception was really on the frontier of Christian, Moslem Europe.

TT   It was the great translating school at Toledo in Spain
where ancient texts were turned from Greek (which Europe had forgotten)
through Arabic and Hebrew into Latin.
From there the ancient world was rediscovered.

MM   And when natural genius was supported by well spent Medici money,
we have what we see around us.

EE   So, who are we going to start with?

PP   You can see the work of Giotto across the square in front of us.
And before that I'd like to introduce a hero of a very exceptional kind.
Born into a wealthy mediaeval family
he brought something new to the lives of all of us.

Baptistry Giotto's Tower

EE   Come on. Stop teasing. Give us a clue!
Who are you talking about and what did he do?

PP It's hard to explain exactly.
I think Francis taught us that believing is joy, not duty.
I think he gave voice to a new relationship between man,
God and the created world.
Can you show me that postcard again? I think his spirit moved us
away from the stern, inflexible, judging attitudes you see in those mosaics
into an appreciation of the good things of Nature.

TT The musician could open his ears to the song of the birds,
not just the solemn chanting of monks.
The sculptor could delight in children dancing in the garden,
not just the stern gaze and stiff postures of distant apostles.

MM Here come the coffees - and who ordered mineral water?

PP Now, look across the piazza at the slender black and white
of Giotto's bell tower.

AA The tower, like the Cathedral behind it, on which he also worked,
wasn't finished until after his death,
but it's what Giotto did for painting, - which is a way we see life,
that has brought us here.

PP Remember, he began his career working with mosaics,
and apprenticed to a Master of icons,
a style from a mediaeval world completely encrusted in tradition.
Giotto's genius was to take the contemporary story of St. Francis
and paint murals which brought his teaching vividly alive.
Giotto discovered so much we take for granted in painting now.

GG I'm beginning to look at those pictures with new eyes.

AA Do you see how he indicates authentic backgrounds from a few details?
And shows the human figures moving,
so that we follow, on the flat surface of a wall,
as Francis preaches to his brothers and sisters of the fields.

PP St. Francis and Giotto gave the world new ways of thinking and seeing.
Their joy in life opens the door of expression
for the great artistic outpouring of the High Renaissance.

TT We've got a lot of filming to do here, don't you think?

EE I'll get the bill, and we'll make a start.

Act 3 Key phrases Find and underline :-

Even more importantly for us...
Very briefly, that's the story...
While we're on the subject...
There's nothing to match these towers...
Europe was probably more internationally minded...
The political and economic realities of life...
A few quick witted citizens...
Giotto discovered so much we take for granted...

Phonology specials

Thistle gate shines whiter than the stream.
On the Great wall, a thousand miles of moonlight.
Gold for splendour, for adornment, for eternity.
The hinges creak, our footsteps echo in the nave...
The musician could open his ears to the song of the birds,
not just the solemn chanting of monks.
Here come the coffees - and who ordered mineral water?

Vocabulary Hunt

Put these words into sentences of your own.
alloy . plunder . impetus .
unforseen . stalemate . stern

Using your senses

Feel the romance of the Great Wall. It stretches into the distant hills. See the flags streaming in the wind and hear the wild bugle calls.

Walk across the cobbled streets and into the cathedral. How dark is it? Are there candles? Can you smell incense? Does your cathedral have beautiful stained glass windows? Sit quietly. Are the monks chanting?

Sit at a pavement cafe in Florence. There's bright sunshine and shadow. Enjoy the movement and chatter of locals and tourists against the background of the wonderful Renaissance palaces and churches. Here comes the waiter.

Enjoy your ice cream!

"Hands on" experiences...

Have a good look at your "Materials collection".
Handle different metals. Polish something made of gold.
Listen to monks chanting.
Colour in some stained glass window designs.

Can you explain please ....

i) TT's comment about Europe being more "internationally minded" in the early Middle Ages.
ii) why Florence was a catalyst for the Renaissance? Have other cities had a similar role at other times in history?

Mini role plays

i) MM and EE - It is 1000 BC. You are the commercial and technical advisors to a relatively conservative community using stone tools. Convince them of the need to change to "modern materials" as soon as possible.

ii) PP - It is 1190AD. You have recently returned from a 'holiday of a lifetime visit' to a great cathedral city. Describe the experience to your neighbours in your small wood and mud built village.

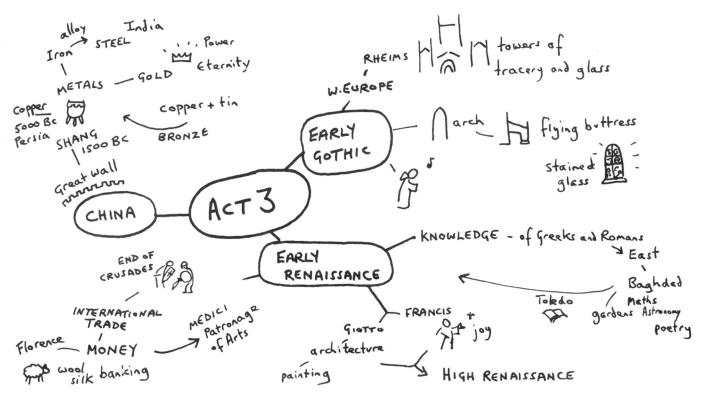

Act 4

Scene 1   At breakfast

MM   Did you sleep well?

PP   Yes thanks, - but with a head full of impressions,
East Africa, the Middle East, Greece, China,
the Incas, the Roman Empire, Mediaeval France,
we've certainly covered some ground so far!

MM   'Morning. How are you feeling?

EE   A bit rough actually. I've got a frog in my throat.

PP   Ah. There's the phone. I'll get it.
Hello.

TT   Sorry not to be with you yet.
I've been held up.
I went to see an aunt in hospital.
She had a transplant operation recently.
She's making an excellent recovery
- wonderful what they can do nowadays.
I was ringing to find out where we're going next
and I'll join you direct.

AA   Cough sweets..... transplant operations..... we're clearly on a medical theme.

GG   Can I suggest a trip to Switzerland?
Not the stereotype of cuckoo clocks and numbered accounts,
but to enjoy some quite radical thinking - and action.

TT   Sounds good to me. Where exactly are we going?

GG   Let's meet in the square outside Basle Cathedral.

TT   Fine. See you there.

Scene 2   Basle - an old Apothecary's shop

PP   How's your throat now?

EE   Much better thanks. These menthol pastils are doing the trick.

GG   I'd like to introduce you to a very colourful relative
who spent a lifetime battling
against the fossilised tradition of the medical profession.
The mediaeval alchemists had taken the Greek idea of four elements
- earth, air, fire and water,
and developed a theory which saw a relationship between
the microcosm of the human body and the macrocosm of Nature.

TT   You've lost me I'm afraid.

AA   I'm not sure I'm with you either. Can you give us some examples?

GG   Certainly. A volcano is like a boil on a grand scale.
A fit of weeping is a miniature version of a rainstorm.
They believed that all metals grew inside the earth
and that everything - including human bodies
consisted of the two main elements, mercury and sulphur.

AA   What a terrible hodge podge of theories!

GG   Yes. And it held science and medicine in a strangle hold.
The physician was a learned academic
who read out of a large and ancient book
while an assistant did what he was told to the body of the poor patient.

AA   Then a hard drinking, womanising, controversial figure,
Paracelsus bursts on to the scene.
He was the first man to recognise an industrial disease.
He won the friendship of Erasmus by curing Frobenius the printer.
He also found a cure for the terrible scourge of syphilis.
And here, just outside the Munster in Basle, in 1527,
he publicly burned an ancient text book by followers of Aristotle.
The thousand year grip of the old alchemy was broken
and we were on the way again to chemistry
and an understanding of life.

MM   It sounds to me as if we're seeing how scientific discovery
flows from the impact of a powerful personality.

PP   You mentioned printing in passing.
We see a great coming together of the ideas of the Reformation
and the powerful new tool for spreading them.

AA   That's right. A great wind of change was starting to blow in Europe.
Luther had made his dramatic challenge in 1517.
Paracelsus was upsetting the establishment
and making himself highly unpopular
by overturning the accepted procedures of medicine.

EE   Then in 1543, Nicolaus Copernicus
really got the scientific establishment by the ears!

TT   Hold on a moment. Are we on to a new subject?
Is there going to be time for some skiing before we move?

EE   Skiing? Sorry - we're due back in Italy again.
Let's get going. I'll give you some background on the way.

Scene 3 Venice

GG   Have you ever been on a gondola before?
It's an interesting exercise in balance!

AA   It's quite a sight to see the city,
which we know so well from pictures,
shimmering serenely in the sun.

PP   Those colours, pinks, violets, blues .....
Can I borrow your binoculars please?
I want to try and identify some of the landmarks.

MM   Mind you don't rock the boat.
That water doesn't look very inviting!

EE   Meanwhile, we should enter the mediaeval mind for a while.
Ptolemy's astronomy and Aristotle's mechanics
represented the Greek view of the natural order of things.
Over the centuries the Church had accepted as an article of faith
that the earth was the centre of the Universe
and the heavenly host marched around it.
It was as if Ptolemy's system had been invented
not by a Levantine Greek, but by the Almighty Himself.

TT   And I suppose you could say that astronomy was the first science?

EE   Yes. It guides us through the cycle of the seasons.
Think of the Babylonians, the Egyptians,
the Mayans with their complex calendars .....

AA   The mediaeval world saw the heavens
as a wonderful construction of planets circling the earth.

EE   Copernicus studied this model and found it didn't fit mathematically.
And then he asked one of these simple questions of genius.
'What would the system look like from another viewpoint?'
If we took, say, the sun as the centre and not the earth.
And now the model worked!
But at the expense of theological confusion.
He called his book the 'Revolution of the Heavenly orbs.'
'Revolution' just means 'turning in a circle',
but from Copernicus on, it also means - violent change!

TT   You get a completely different viewpoint of a place
from being on the water.

PP   Thanks for the binoculars. You can see revellers in St. Mark's square
still wearing their carnival masks.

GG   The city seems to be a great magnet for the curious of the world.

MM   Mmm. That at least hasn't changed in four hundred years.
Two great men were born in 1564.

AA   Don't tell me. Let me guess.
One was Shakespeare, I think.
Could the other one have been Gallileo?

PP   Yes. And it's no coincidence that when Shakespeare writes about power
he twice brings the scene for the play to Venice.
'The Merchant of Venice,' of course, and also the tragic 'Othello.'

MM   That's because in 1600 the Mediterranean was still the centre of the world
and Venice was the hub of the Mediterranean.
In a state of seafaring traders
Gallileo's greatly improved telescope won him fame and status.

EE   He then stepped up the magnification
and turned it into a means of research.
He built an instrument, did experiments, published the results.

PP   Those first maps of the moon are an eye opener.

EE   He also discovered the moons of Jupiter and,
demonstrated that Copernicus's powerful guess was right.

TT   And how did the 'powers that be' react to the ending of the Plotemaic picture?

EE   With condemnation. Remember, this was the time of the Counter Reformation.

AA   For the rest of his life Galileo faced prosecution from the Inquisition.
Censure, trial, the instruments of torture,
and eventually this dissident scientist was humiliated and forced to recant.

GG   And what effect did that have on the intellectual climate?

EE   An important one. The Catholic scientists were silenced.
From that point on the scientific revolution moved to Northern Europe.
Gallileo died, a prisoner in his house in 1642.
On Christmas Day that year, in England, Isaac Newton was born.

Scene 4 Cambridge - Trinity College Library

EE   We're going to have to tiptoe round the Library.

TT   Is this where Newton did his research?

EE   Some of it, certainly. He was made Professor of Mathematics in Cambridge
at the age of twenty six!

MM   We'll have to keep our voices down ... whisper.

TT   Yes, we don't want to wake the chap dozing over there!

PP   I'm sure, if you woke him, he'd say he closed his eyes to concentrate!

GG   Is there any truth in the story of the apple
giving him inspiration for the theory of gravity?

EE   It's a nice picture, isn't it.
The young mathematical genius, sitting under a tree in the orchard ....
an apple hits him on the head and he discovers the law that binds the universe!

TT   Well, we know something about
the right and left hemisphere of the brain these days.
Perhaps it really was a flash of inspiration
followed by many hours of calculation!

EE   Newton worked out the formulae which hold the planets in their orbits.
As with Pythagoras, the mathematical structure,
the harmony within Nature, is suddenly made visible.

AA   Having made such a breakthrough at such a young age,
what did Newton do with the rest of his life?

EE   Reach up and get that first edition,
the leather bound volume to the left of the top shelf.

GG   Are these Newton's experiments?

EE   Yes. He shut himself in a dark room for a while,
formulated theories, tested them against alternatives,
and demonstrated that white light consists of separate colours.
He made huge strides in understanding gravity, light, time and space
and he became President of the Royal Society.

MM   We've seen before how economic pressures generate a spirit of the age.
In Newton's time the sea faring world
demanded better telescopes, reliable clocks .....
The meridian line at the Greenwich Observatory
provided sailors with a fixed mark in their storm tossed world.

PP   Newton himself, the intellectual giant of the age
seemed to have been a lonely man, dissatisfied to the end.
He wrote of himself, 'I do not know what I may appear to the world,
but to myself I seem to have been only like a boy playing on the seashore
and diverting myself in now and then finding a smoother pebble
or a prettier shell than the ordinary
while the great ocean of truth lay all undiscovered before me.'

AA   Oh no!

TT   What's the matter?

AA   I've just realised I haven't got my folder of notes.

TT   When did you last have them?

AA   I don't remember having them in Venice.
          I must have left them in the hotel in Basle.

TT   Don't worry. It would be very appropriate
          to call on another relative - in Bern this time.

GG   But I could do with a cup of tea, and,
          how about some apple pie before we go?

Scene 5 The Clock Tower in Bern

AA   You were talking about the development of clocks.
          Now here's a really spectacular example!

TT   Shall we wait till it strikes?

EE   Certainly. And here's something to think about while we wait.
          The universe of Newton ticked on without a hitch for two hundred years.
          Yet here, not two hundred metres from this Clock Tower,
          lived another young man who thrust us into the present era.

PP   Mind out! Here comes a tram. We'd better move.

MM   It's probably a direct descendant of the tram
          that Einstein caught every day on his way to work!

EE   As Copernicus took the sun as a startling new viewpoint for the universe,
          Einstein asked 'What would the universe look like
          if I were riding on a beam of light?'

$$E = MC^2$$

          For Newton, time and space were absolutes.
          Einstein reasoned that what you see and what I see,
          is different, relative to our place and speed.
          He'd finish a day at the Patent Office,
          have a cigar and a chat at the cafe over there,
          and go home to work on 'The electrodynamics of moving bodies'.

MM   As I understand it, Einstein related light to time,
          time to space, energy to matter, space to gravitation.

GG   That's an extraordinary range of achievement, isn't it?
          What was he like as a person do you think?

EE   A mild mannered genius.
          Completely without vanity.

AA   He turned down an invitation to become President of Israel, didn't he?

EE   That's right.
          At the end of his life, wearing his old jersey
          and his slippers with no socks, he'd lecture at Cambridge
          on the connection between gravitation, electricity, magnetism.
          So his insights pushed ajar the door to the atomic age .....

PP   That's a sombre but exciting place to pause.

TT   I suggest that next we catch up on the music scene,
          and also see the building blocks of life.

GG   Enjoy the rest of the day. There's lots in store tomorrow!

Act 4

Key phrases Find and underline :-

I was ringing to find out...
I'm not sure I'm with you.
It sounds to me as if...
You mentioned printing in passing...
I suppose you could say that...
It's no coincidence that when Shakespeare writes about power...
And what effect did that have?
Is there any truth in the story...
That's an extraordinary range of achievements...

Phonology specials

The city shimmering serenely in the sun.
Mind you don't rock the boat.
We'll have to keep our voices down....whisper.
That's a sombre but exciting place to pause.
What's the matter?

Vocabulary Hunt Find phrases in the text for ...

an annoying little cough -
causing disagreement -
colloquial reference to the Establishment -
a very important discovery -
a small problem -

Using your senses

In the Apothecary's shop, take a handful of dried herbs, crush them, and breathe in deeply. Even the smell clears your head and makes you feel good.

You are in a gondola in Venice. Feel it rocking gently. Hear the splash of water against the boat. It sparkles in the sunlight. Hear the shouts of gondoliers. On either side of you are elegant, faded palaces. You will soon have a wonderful view of St. Mark's and the City - serene in the calm air.

Sit for some time in this Cambridge library. Around you are shelves of dark wood - full of priceless manuscripts. Scholars are carefully examining the delicate pages. It is very, very quiet. Let your mind explore, and remember the learning experiences which have been of most value to you.

"Hands on" experiences...

Have a good look at your "Materials collection".
Make a display of herbs / flowers in medicinal / culinary use today.
Do some "gravity proving" experiments (you can eat the apple afterwards !).
Use a telescope or binoculars.
Use a prism to break light into colours.

To think about

Act 3 Scene 4 and Act 4 Scene 3. Both highlight religious attitudes and
their impact on the spiritual, intellectual and aesthetic climate of those times.
What other examples can you think of? Is the point equally true today?

Excuse me. Can you explain..

    i)   the difference between the mediaeval world view and what Paracelsus and Copernicus said?

    ii)   the contribution of Newton and Einstein to our understanding of science?

    iii)   the connection between Gallileo and the American space programme?

Mini role plays

The greatest scientific auction ever! Working in pairs "bring" an item which has contributed to science (for example, the apple that fell on Newton's head), present it, and its significance, to the group. Take a vote for the most important item.

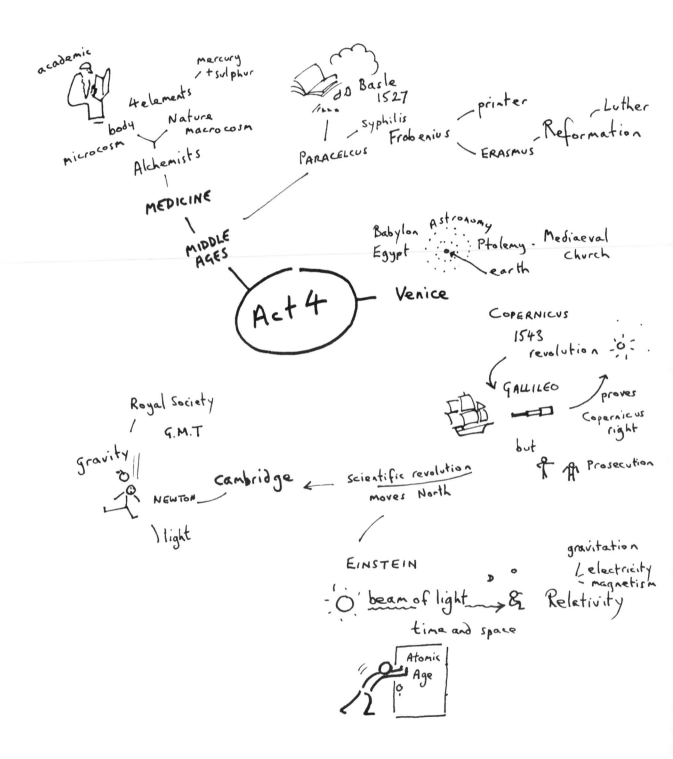

Act 5

Scene 1 Shropshire, England

AA   We must be about in the middle of the bridge, don't you think?
Grip the iron railings firmly - it'll help you feel why
this bridge is part of all our heritage.

GG   It's elegant, certainly, and fairly high,
but what other significance does it have?

EE   This is Ironbridge - **the** iron bridge.
A beautiful symbol of the power of Nature
put to the service of mankind.

PP   You're very lyrical about such a functional object, aren't you?

EE   Yes, but let me explain why.
The England of Newton - like the rest of the eighteenth century world,
was a village based society.
Within two generations the Industrial Revolution changed that scene completely.

TT   The Golden Age gave way to smog and factory work, I suppose.

MM   I wouldn't agree with you there.
There never was a Golden Age for our relatives the farm workers.
Life had always been a dawn to dusk struggle against poverty.
And if it hadn't been for the Industrial Revolution,
life would still be like that for us.

EE   In a remarkable explosion of engineering talent
our engineering relatives, practical men with little formal education,
dug mines, built canals and bridges,
and powered machines to meet the demands of expanding trade.

AA   The fiery red skies over the furnaces of this valley
forged men into industrial communities,
just as they forged the iron for this bridge in 1779.

PP   So what's the link between trade, engineering and the ascent of Man?

MM   The barges didn't carry luxury goods from the factories to the world .
They carried pots and pans, and bales of cloth, and boxes of ribbons.
All the things to raise the standard of living of ordinary people.

AA   Life for the poor was still hard certainly,
and industrialisation had a sordid side,
but here was a new concept, science with a social conscience.

EE   Wedgewood made porcelain masterpieces for Catherine the Great of Russia
but the table-ware from his factory also transformed
the kitchens of the working class.

MM   Men like him, Priestley the chemist, Boulton and Watt with steam engines,
- held a revolutionary doctrine that material decency was the right of everyone.

EE   A Cornish wrestler, Trevethick mounted Watt's beam engine on wheels,
and the Railway Age had arrived!

PP   Do you know Turner's painting of a steam locomotive?
The clouds of smoke, the sparks, the pounding pistons.
You can feel the excitement of a world of communication opening up.

TT   Is it my imagination or was that a spot of rain?

CC   I think you're right.
          Our next stop is steamy in a different way,   you'll need jungle gear.

Scene 2 Brazil

AA   You're right. It is hot and steamy!
         Just listen to the noise ..... parrots squawking .....
         all kinds of insects ..... and the colours are unbelievable.
         Careful where you step! The forest floor is alive with small creatures.

GG   Now, quiz time. Who do you think wrote this?
         'One day in tearing off some old bark I saw two rare beetles
         and seized one in each hand:
         then I saw a third and new kind which I couldn't bear to lose,
         so I popped the one I held in my right hand into my mouth!'

EE   Obviously someone with a passion for his work!

GG   Very much so. Darwin's visit here in 1831
         convinced him that species which are isolated from each other
         develop in different ways.
         Also that as animals compete for limited food supplies
         the weak die off,
         and those which adapt best to their environment
         breed and develop new species.

PP   There are certainly some remarkable adaptations here, aren't there?
         Look at the protective camouflage on the wings of that butterfly!

AA   This process of natural selection has been called
         "the single most important scientific advance of the nineteenth century",
         but I'm not sure why.

MM   As I see it, it demonstrates that the living world is in constant change.

PP   The physical laws governing the world haven't changed in ten million years,
         but if Darwin is right we all trace our origins back to the very beginnings of life.

TT   And evolution accounts for the incredible diversity we see around us.

GG   Darwin hesitated twenty years
         before finally publishing 'the Origin of Species,' in 1859.
         He knew his ideas would produce the same sort of shock wave
         as those of Copernicus had done earlier.

MM   Does anyone else feel itchy?

EE   I do. I could do with a good shower and a change of clothes!

Scene 3 Vienna

PP   Well, this is quite a contrast to our last visit!
         Glittering chandeliers, the audience very elegant in evening dress ....

MM   We haven't heard from our musical relatives recently .
         It's about time we caught up on their contribution.

TT   We've got a few moments before the concert starts.
Take this Stradivarius in your hands .....
touch the polished chestnut brown of the body ....
test the balance of the bow in your right hand .....
and now play a note and let it rise, linger, and fade away.

GG   If I remember rightly we had our last musical experience in Rheims Cathedral ....

AA   At that time there were very few instruments, I believe,
and until Guido of Arrezzo, no standard way of writing notes.
Keyboard instruments developed from the early prototypes he used,
and the craftsmen of Cremona created superb violins
like the one you're holding.

GG   Cremona? So Renaissance Italy was a power house of music
as well as painting and sculpture?

TT   That's right.
Pallestrina began the move which made instrumental music acceptable,
and Monteverdi turned a group of musicians into an orchestra.
Do you remember looking at St. Mark's in Venice through the binoculars?
Monteverdi was Choir Master there in the 1640's.

MM   Can you pass me the programme please?
There's no Monteverdi, is there?

AA   No, we've actually come to Vienna to listen to Mozart.

TT   But first we should thank the man who laid the foundations.
It's well worth retelling the story
of how young Johann Sebastian was brought up by an older brother
who wouldn't let him borrow his collection of harpsichord manuscripts.
So every night for six months the boy would creep out of bed,
tiptoe to the cabinet and copy music by the light of the moon.
Just as he had almost finished,
his brother caught him, beat him, and destroyed his treasures.
Those six months, sadly, ruined Bach's eyesight
but could not quench his spirit and creative output.
His life was a humble struggle to satisfy insensitive employers
and he never received recognition or wealth as a reward,
but he gave us jewels of technical and spiritual excellence
like the Matthew Passion and the Brandenburg Concertos.

EE   Would you agree with me that in great creative achievements,
whether they are Giotto's frescoes, or Bach's music,
- or James Watt's steam engine,
there is a logical elegance which is completely satisfying?

PP   Bach, Handel and Hayden, what pleasure they give.
And Mozart who played for the Emperor when he was six,
poured out operas, symphonies, requiems of unmatched harmony and delight,
and was buried in a pauper's grave by the age of thirty six.

AA   The orchestra are tuning up and, here comes the conductor. . . .

Scene 4   The Monastery of Brno, Czechoslovakia

EE   This is very pleasant. The sun warm on the brick walls,
       the scent of honeysuckle and murmur of bees.
       What are you looking at so intently?

PP   Just a few pea pods. Open one ...
       I picked them from the plants growing over there.

GG   I was reminded, when we were in Vienna,
       that Gregor Mendel studied there - failed his teaching exams
       and retired here in disgrace to become a monk.
       But it was in Vienna he became interested in biology .
       That triggered his eight years of secret study in this garden.

AA   I'm afraid you'll have to put us in the picture a bit more.

MM   I'm not sure what Mendel did
       let alone why his studies had to be secret!

GG   I'll start with that point first.
       Rather like the Counter Reformation of Gallileo's time,
       the Imperial Austrian Empire in the 1880's
       took a very dim view of experimental science
       and certalnly Gregor's fellow monks would have been extremely suspicious
       if they'd known what he was up to.
       Now, to come back to your original question.
       Take some black paint and some white paint.
       Mix it. What do you get?

MM   Grey paint.

GG   Right. Take a hot liquid and a cold liquid.
       Mix them. What do you get?

MM   A warm liquid.

GG   Right. Take one of these tall pea plants, and a short one.
       Cross fertilize them, and what do you get?

MM   A pea of medium height, I suppose?

GG   Wrong.
       In every four such matings, three plants will be tall, and one short.
       Mendel's eight years of carefully documented research
       cracked the code governing heredity.
       He recognised that two is the magic number in fertilization,
       that each gene contributes characteristics
       and that one gene will be dominant.

AA   Of course, at that time no one had heard of genes, or chromosomes.

GG   No. Mendel's papers were burned on his death
       and his work forgotten for thirty years.
       When it was rediscovered in 1900
       the study of genetics became the adventure story of the century.

PP   I see what you mean. What could be more exciting than unravelling
       how the message of inheritance is passed from one generation to the next?

AA   And the deciphering of the structure of DNA in 1953.

GG   Well, we've moved from the chance crossing of wild grasses
to an understanding of the genetic code of life!

MM   I don't know about you, but I've enjoyed following the trail
from flint tools to nuclear reactors and the computer revolution.

TT   For me it's been a journey from the structure of the arch
to the structure of the universe!

PP   Of course, the story isn't finished,
but has anyone any suggestions as to how we end our film?

EE   One of the things I've appreciated in these journeys is that our relatives,
and we ourselves, are wonderful instruments for learning!

AA   Yes, and that knowledge isn't just a note book full of facts.

TT   Let's stay in the serenity of this little garden
with the piles of freshly cut grass
and the blossom already on the trees,
but let's also look over the wall.

GG   I'm glad you said that
because what happens in Sudan, the rain forests, Iraq,
that's the test for all of us.

AA   You're absolutely right.
Our civilisation, our age, hasn't been given any promise of permanence
that wasn't given to the vanished cultures of the past.

MM   It's our courage and integrity that's in question now,
and that's a matter of intellectual and emotional commitment.

PP   Our relatives have shown us quite a lot of where we've been.

EE   It's up to us, now, to take a hand in shaping where we go!

Act 5
Key phrases - Find and underline :-

What other significance does it have?
Within two generations...
If it hadn't been for the Industrial Revolution...
So what's the link between...?
Evolution accounts for the incredible diversity...
It's about time we caught up on...
It's well worth retelling...
To come back to your original question...
I'm afraid you'll have to put us in the picture a bit more.

Phonology specials

The clouds of smoke, the sparks, the pounding pistons.
Is it my imagination, or was that a spot of rain?
Careful where you step. The forest floor is alive with small insects.
Play a note and let it rise, linger, and fade away.
For me, it's been a journey from the structure of the arch,
to the structure of the universe.

Vocabulary hunt - Complete the following :-

The Golden Age...

Wedgewood made...

Does anyone else..

His life was..

The Imperial Austrian Empire took............................

It's up to us now to...

Using your senses

It's hot and humid, but allow your eyes to take in the incredible variety of brilliant colours - birds, butterflies. There's the smell of vegetation all around - and let your ears tune in to the different sounds of the rain forest.

Put on your best evening clothes and take the companion of your choice to this musical gala. Look around at the magnificence of the concert hall and the elegance of the audience. Settle comfortably as the sublime music charms your senses. This will be a beautiful experience.

You have travelled to wonderful places, met creative people, enjoyed exciting experiences. Take time now to sit quietly and let your 'mental home movie' run through again. Travel from Africa to the caves in Spain, and the ancient Middle East. Visit Egypt, Greece and the Incas of the Andes. Walk on the Great Wall, around the Mediaeval Cathedral, and Renaissance Italy. Take another handful of the Apothecary's herbs, enjoy a gondola trip, and pause in the library. Think of the industrial revolution, and wonder at the rainforest. Let the music play again...and feel enriched by our heritage, and challenged by our future.

"Hands on" experiences...

Have a good look at your "Materials collection"
Listen to some Bach or Mozart.
Look for a likeness in photos between yourself and your grandparents / parents.

Excuse me. Can you explain...

i)   the connection between GG's description of emmer (Act 1 Scene 3),
        Gregor Mendel, and DNA?
ii)   why Darwin's theory caused such a 'shock wave'?

To think about

i) What different roles has music had in Relatively Speaking (Act 1.1, Act 3.2, etc). Are there other roles we haven't mentioned?

ii) What other scene would you like to add to this 'Relatively Speaking' account of the development of ideas?

Mini role plays

i) AA, MM. It is 1800. Persuade the population of an English village that it is in their interests that you build an industrial factory on their land. Everyone else - are you happy about the proposal?

ii) Choose any scene from Relatively Speaking and produce it as a drama. Use the text as a starting point, and as many 'props' as possible.

Teaching Notes

The Course gives an active overview of key ideas which have shaped civilisation. Indeed, the original springboard for the course was Dr Jacob Bronowski's marvellous BBC series entitled 'The Ascent of Man' which did so much to make the complex fields of science, arts, religion and philosophy accessible to the general public. A copy of the book of that series (ISBN 0-563170-64-6) is of great value as additional reading.

The course provides excellent language work, fascinating general knowledge, and challenging discussion starters on the development of issues which affect our life today.

The course format. 'Relatively Speaking' is a drama with six characters. An on-going role play in which participants visit many areas of the world for the purpose of making a film about civilisation. The five Acts are divided into scenes and each Act is followed by a memory map and exercises.

Suggested procedure. All the course participants choose a surname from the list given on page 3, and also choose a first name to match it, i.e. Tanya Timpani, Patrick Penandink. With over six participants, more than one person will choose the same family name. This is actually good for the group dynamic as several members of the same family will then be "relatives" and have to work out their "relationship".

Use the **list of Ancillary Materials** on page 39 to collect appropiate items for enriching the class environment with pictures, posters, objects, music and sound effects, smells, tastes etc. (The class can help you collect)

'Relatively Speaking' is written as a Suggestopedic text. If used in this way the following pattern would be recommended.

- An Introduction to the content of the Act.
- The Act read to classical music followed by a comprehension check.
- The Act read to Baroque music.
- Activations (the longest stage).

The Introduction:

Place the items from the materials list around the room and invite participants to choose something and say a few words about it. Alternatively present the items yourself, linking them into story, or direct each student to some particular thing i.e. Find a picture of the bearded man who wrote 'Origin of Species'. Another technique is to have each student contribute an item from around the room, and then play 'Kim's Game' (Pelmanism). All this raises anticipation and plants memory traces of names and ideas which will prove useful when the learners meet the text.

Concert 1: Read the text to classical music (or use the cassette until you have the confidence to do this). The students mark anything of particular interest or which they wish to ask about.

Checking: In small groups students talk through the text, helping one another with comprehension. This can be a very creative activity. The teacher unobtrusively monitors - but only comments if asked.

Concert 2: Read the text again, this time to Baroque music. Students sit in a relaxed but alert position, probably with closed eyes, and just listen. This is a good phase on which to either complete a lesson or to open a new one.

Activations: After a suitable break, read out the 'Key phrases'. Students **underline** them in colour in the text. (This has the benefit of giving a lot of **peripheral reading**).

Use body language and plenty of expression to drill the '**phonology specials**' which contain many good examples of **intonation** patterns and **pronunciation** points.
Use a variety of **reading drills, repetition, pair work**, to thoroughly familiarise students with the text.
Students should highlight their personal character roles and, working in a group of six, prepare a lively **dramatized reading** of one or more scenes.
Students use the **Memory Maps** to **summarise the information** contained in the Act.
In many cases, participants will want to use the content as a **discussion** starter for their own ideas and knowledge.
Bring the powers of visualisation into operation with the '**Use your senses**' sections. These can be extended as guided visualisation exercises to help participants enter into the spirit of the situation.
Have some active fun - and share ideas - using the 'hands on' experiences section. Remember that the more **ancillary materials** available, the better.
Recycle the language with the mini roleplays - many of them are deliberately light - hearted.
The **cultural context** chart will be a useful reference point as you move from scene to scene.

In this way participants in '**Relatively Speaking**' will rapidly benefit from the rich language input, the communicative practice, and the creative opportunities developed through the Course.

Timing.   As a guideline it is suggested that 3 - 4 hours is spent on each Act. If you are following the suggestopedic approach :- The Introduction , Concert 1 , Checking , and Concert 2 stages will take at least 20 minutes each , and the Activations will take at least an hour and a half , especially if you have brought plenty of ancillary visual material into the room and encourage discussion.

Ancillary Materials list

These are the sort of items which will provide extra stimulus by creating a rich visual and tangible learning environment.
Postcards / posters / toys / books / maps / food / realia..... the more the merrier!

Act 1 pictures: Kenya . fossils . pole vaulter . lions . stone tools .
reindeer . snow and ice . cave paintings . cave dwellers . Middle East agriculture .
ancient tools -   weaving etc., a well. a plough . goats / oxen

items :   world map . N.Africa map . toy animals . fossils .
stone tools . torch . corn . cornflakes . something with wheels

Act 2 pictures: Greek island . Egyptian sculpture and painting .
Assyrian carving . hieroglyphics . Greek temple .
Andes . Aztec cities . molecules . stone arches .   Roman arches / aquaduct

items :   grapes . stringed instrument . maths book . clay or
plasticine for modelling.   Cassette of flute music from the Andes.

Act 3 pictures: Great Wall of China . Chinese bronze pots . atoms / crystals .
gold ornaments . Mediaeval cathedral . stained glass windows . Florence . Giotto's tower .
Byzantine mosaics . Arab culture . Moorish garden. manuscript illustration .
Giotto frescoes . Tuscany

items :   cassette of Gregorian chant . gold ring . metal tools
stained glass window colouring book.

Act 4 pictures: Switzerland . Basle . Venice - St. Mark's / gondolas .
Gallileo . The moon. Newton . Cambridge colleges . Bern clock tower . Einstein

items :   masks . telescope . throat medicine . ' Merchant of Venice' .
apple . prism . clock . tram

Act 5 pictures: Ironbridge . industrial revolution . steam engines . early trains
(like the Rocket) . Turner painting - 'Rain, steam & speed'
Brazilian rain forest . bright butterflies / beetles . Darwin .   Vienna . concert hall .violin .
Mozart . Bach .   genetic - fertilization . embryo .walled garden

items :   plate & cup . violin . sheet music . cassette of Bach / Mozart . pea pods

Props for the mini role plays.   Plenty of 'dressing clothes' - hats, scarves,etc. will add to the fun of the role plays.

Use lots of 'props'

Cultural Context Chart

A time-line guide (approximate) to the main events and people mentioned in Relatively Speaking - and a few others.

BC	MIDDLE EAST	AMERICAS	EUROPE	OTHER AREAS

BC
3500

Dawn of Civilisation circa 4000 B.C.

3000 — **Sumer** - city states
- agriculture
- cuneiform

2500 — raiding nomads / stoneage

Egypt - heiroglyphics — **Indus Valley** (India)

pyramids — bronzeage

2000 — **Babylon** - code of laws — **Maya** - textiles — **Minoans** (Crete) — **China** - writing
- libraray — - weaving — - calendar
- astronomy

Abraham - nomad to settler
1500 — Jericho — - bronzes

ironage
1000 — King David (Jerusalem) — **Mycenaens**

500 — **Persian Empire** — **Golden Age of Greece** — Confucius
Socrates — Buddha
Pythageras — **Great Wall of China**
Alexander
Romans

0 AD — Jesus

Han Dynasty (China)

Dark Ages
Celtic Culture
Byzantine Empire
500 — Mohammed

Charlemagne
Mediaeval World
Middle Ages
1000 — Crusades — Gothic — Chinese culture reaches Japan and Korea

Rise of Islam — **Aztecs** (Mexico) — Copernicus — **Ghengis Khan**
Giotto. St. Francis — **Ming Dynasty** (China)
Incas (Peru) — **Renaissance** - Medicis
1500 — **Ottoman Empire** — Galileo. Shakespeare — **Mogul Dynasty** (India)
Voyages of Discovery — Taj Mahal
Refomation — Peter the Great (Russia)
Newton. Bach.
Mendel. Mozart.
Industrial Revolution — Rise of The U.S.A.
2000 — Darwin. Einstein — **Atomic Age**